THE AMERICAN DREAM!

The USA won the World Cup for the fourth time at the last tournament in 2019 — beating Netherlands 2-0 in the final!

MATCH OF THE DAY

WELCOME!

G'DAY, MATES! It's time to get hyped for the Women's World Cup. Join us on an incredible journey down under as we look at the two host nations, all 32 teams and the biggest stars who'll be on show this summer. It's going to be wild!

WHAT'S IN YOUR MOTD MA

WOMEN'S WORLD CUP WINNERS!

This is the ninth Women's World Cup — but who won the previous ones?

1991	**USA**	🇺🇸
1995	**NORWAY**	
1999	**USA**	🇺🇸
2003	**GERMANY**	
2007	**GERMANY**	
2011	**JAPAN**	
2015	**USA**	🇺🇸
2019	**USA**	🇺🇸
2023?	_Spain_	

Who do you think will win it? Write their name and colour their flag!

ANNUAL?

96 PAGES OF FOOTY FUN!

WORLD CUP GROUP GUIDES!

51

76

EPIC QUIZ ZONE!

WORLD CUP HERO POSTERS!

WELCOME TO

For the first time ever, two nations will host the Women's World Cup, Australia and New Zealand. Check out the countries, the cities, the stadiums... and the critters!

FACT FILE
AUSTRALIA

Capital city: Canberra
Population: 26 million
Money: Australian dollar
National colours: Gold and green
National animals: Kangaroo and emu
Women's team nickname: The Matildas
Top player: Sam Kerr
Fun fact: Australia isn't just a country — it's a whole continent on its own!

WOW!
The saltwater crocodile is the largest living reptile!

ULURU
A huge sacred sandstone rock!

WOW!
Aussie superstar Sam Kerr made her debut for Perth Glory at age 15!

PERTH

STADIUM: Perth Rectangular Stadium
CAPACITY: 20,000
The stadium was once nicknamed the Oval. The host city will stage five group games!

WOW!
Perth is the only place where quokkas live in the wild — there are 10,000 near the city!

ADELAIDE

STADIUM: Hindmarsh Stadium
CAPACITY: 15,000
The Hindmarsh may be the smallest stadium but it will welcome some of the biggest teams in the tournament, including Brazil and England!

AUSTRALIA!

WOW!
Brisbane is famous for its big wheel, cakes and koalas. It has the largest koala sanctuary in the world!

WOW!
Kangaroos can jump nine metres in one bound — that's longer than a double-decker bus!

WOW!
The city of Melbourne was once called Batmania!

CANBERRA
Capital city

BRISBANE

STADIUM: Brisbane Stadium
CAPACITY: 52,250
Nicknamed the Cauldron because of its atmosphere — the Lionesses will play their first match here!

SYDNEY

STADIUM: Sydney Football Stadium
CAPACITY: 42,500
This is the newest host stadium in the tournament — its roof is made from 4,000 pieces of steel!

SYDNEY

STADIUM: Stadium Australia
CAPACITY: 81,500
This is Australia's national stadium. It will stage the tournament final on 20 August. Who will be there?

MELBOURNE

STADIUM: Melbourne Rectangular Stadium
CAPACITY: 30,100
This stadium on the south coast of the country has an unusual honeycomb-style roof!

GROUP GAMES IN AUSTRALIA

GROUP B
Australia
Republic of Ireland
Nigeria
Canada

GROUP D
England
Haiti
Denmark
China

GROUP F
France
Jamaica
Brazil
Panama

GROUP H
Germany
Morocco
Colombia
South Korea

TURN OVER FOR NEW ZEALAND!

WELCOME TO

FACT FILE
NEW ZEALAND

Capital City: Wellington
Population: 5.2 million
Money: New Zealand dollar
Languages: English and Maori
National colours: Black, red and white
National symbol: Silver fern
National animal: Kiwi bird
Women's team nickname: Football Ferns
Top women's player: Ali Riley
Fun fact: New Zealand's Maori name is Aotearoa — it means 'Land of the long white cloud'.

WANT TO SAY HELLO IN NEW ZEALAND? THE MAORI WORD IS 'KIA ORA'!

AUCKLAND

STADIUM: Eden Park
CAPACITY: 46,350
Eden Park is New Zealand's national stadium. It will stage the opening ceremony and the first game!

WOW!
Half of the world's whale species can be found in the waters around New Zealand!

WOW!
Silver Ferns captain Ali Riley has played for Chelsea and Bayern Munich!

WOW!
There are five sheep for every person in New Zealand!

CHRISTCH

WOW!
Dunedin is famous for penguins. You'll spot rare yellow-eyed penguins on the coast!

NEW ZEALAND!

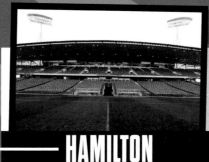

HAMILTON

STADIUM: Waikato **CAPACITY:** 23,100
Players must enter the Waikato stadium through the Whatanoa Gateway — a Maori tradition before battle!

WELLINGTON

STADIUM: Wellington Regional Stadium
CAPACITY: 35,000
The capital's stadium is known as the Cake Tin because of its distinctive shape!

DUNEDIN

STADIUM: Dunedin **CAPACITY:** 28,600
The Dunedin is an eco-friendly stadium — it collects rainwater on its roof to help maintain the pitch!

WELLINGTON
Capital city

WOW!
The Kiwi bird is New Zealand's national animal. It has tiny wings — but it cannot fly!

WOW!
There are 50 volcanoes in New Zealand!

GROUP GAMES IN NEW ZEALAND

GROUP A
New Zealand
Norway
Philippines
Switzerland

GROUP C
Spain
Costa Rica
Zambia
Japan

GROUP E
USA
Vietnam
Netherlands
Portugal

GROUP G
Sweden
South Africa
Italy
Argentina

WOMEN'S WORLD CUP

1895
This is Nettie Honeyball. She started the first recorded British ladies football team!

53,000
By 1920, women's footy was big. More than 50,000 watched the most famous team, Dick, Kerr Ladies — with 10,000 more locked outside!

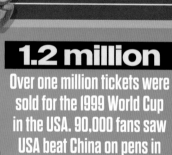

1.2 million
Over one million tickets were sold for the 1999 World Cup in the USA. 90,000 fans saw USA beat China on pens in the final in Pasadena!

£4.6 million
In 2007, the winners took home prize money for the first time — Germany collected the winnings!

4
The USA have bossed the World Cup — they've won it four times!

DID YOU KNOW?
Megan Rapinoe has been a world champ twice with the USA!

17
Brazilian baller Marta is the all-time top scorer at World Cup finals — for men and women — she's bagged 17 goals in total!

REWIND!

The 2023 Women's World Cup will be the biggest ever. Check out how the game has grown with these key dates, stats and facts!

1920

The game went global. The first unofficial international women's game was played between France and England!

50

In 1921, the FA decided that football was 'unsuitable for females' in England — that ban stood for 50 years. In some countries, such as Brazil, women's football was actually made illegal!

BUT THE GIRLS KEPT PLAYING!

DID YOU KNOW?
China gave FIFA this trophy to mark the first Women's World Cup in 1991!

1991

Finally, the first official FIFA women's World Cup took place in China. Only 12 countries took part, games lasted 80 minutes and there was no prize money!

2

Two unofficial women's world tournaments took place in Italy in 1970 and Mexico in 1971. Eight nations entered — and Denmark won both of them!

DID YOU KNOW?
Marta is arguably the GOAT when it comes to women's footy!

13-0

USA smashed Thailand 13-0 in 2019 — the biggest win in Women's World Cup history!

32

There will be 32 countries at the 2023 World Cup, with eight nations making their debut. It will be the biggest Women's World Cup tournament ever!

FLAG QUIZ!

ANSWERS ON p92!

Can you name the 2023 WORLD CUP NATION by their flag? Time to find out!

1
A ITALY
B REPUBLIC OF IRELAND ✓
C ZAMBIA

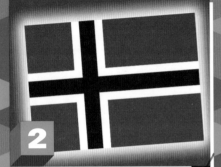

2
A NORWAY ✓
B DENMARK
C VIETNAM

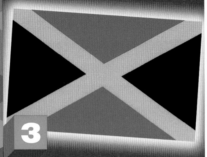

3
A SOUTH AFRICA
B HAITI
C JAMAICA ✓

4
A COLOMBIA
B JAPAN
C SOUTH KOREA ✓

5
A PORTUGAL
B BRAZIL ✓
C ARGENTINA

6
A FRANCE
B MOROCCO
C NIGERIA ✓

7
A SPAIN ✓
B CHINA
C COLOMBIA

8
A AUSTRALIA ✓
B NEW ZEALAND
C PANAMA

9
A COSTA RICA
B SWITZERLAND
C CANADA ✓

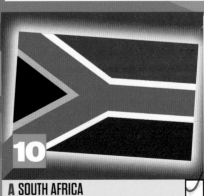

10
A SOUTH AFRICA
B PHILIPPINES
C COSTA RICA

McCABE

REPUBLIC OF IRELAND

FACTFILE

Full name Katie Alison McCabe
Date of birth 21 September 1995 (age 27)
Place of birth Dublin, Ireland
Position Winger **Club** Arsenal

MEET THE

LIONESSES!

England have been on a mega winning run over the past two years. Get to know the top English ballers dreaming of bringing the World Cup home!

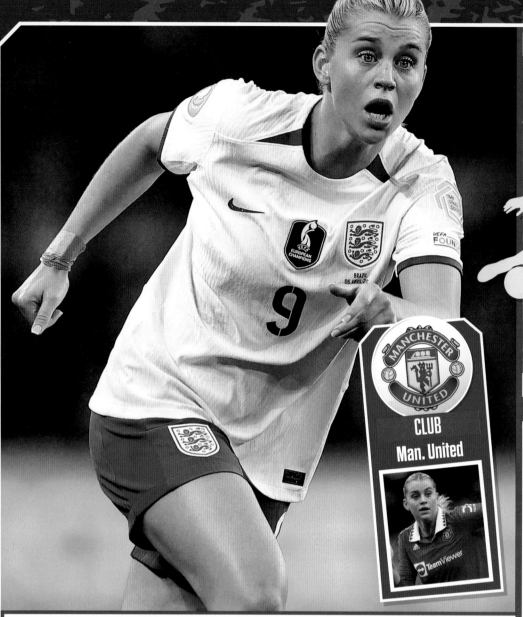

AGE
24

POSITION
STRIKER

TOP MOMENT
Backheel finish v Sweden!

ENGLAND GAMES/GOALS
21/11

CLUB
Man. United

ALESSIA RUSSO
THE GOAL MACHINE!

LETHAL 'LESS IS England's go-to goalscorer. She was a super-sub at Euro 2022, stepping off the bench to decide games, but now she's manager Sarina Wiegman's starting sharpshooter. She's got a magic first touch and uses her speed and strength to dominate!

DID YOU KNOW...
She's best friends with fellow Lioness, Ella Toone!

HER TRADEMARK

PACE AND POWER!

CLUB
Barcelona

AGE

31

POSITION
RIGHT-BACK

TOP MOMENT
Winning the Best FIFA Women's Player 2020!

ENGLAND GAMES/GOALS
104/12

LUCY BRONZE

THE FLYING FULL-BACK!

LUCE HAS PLAYED for the best clubs in the world, alongside the world's flashiest ballers — and has still shone. She's a wicked, modern defender, who loves nipping down the wing to pop in a cross just as much as she loves hitting a perfectly timed tackle!

DID YOU KNOW...

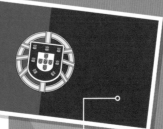

Bronze could have played for Portugal — but she chose the Lionesses!

HER TRADEMARK

OUTSIDE-OF-THE-BOX ROCKET!

CLUB
Chelsea

AGE
29

POSITION
CENTRE-BACK

TOP MOMENT
Top goalscorer at 2022 Arnold Clark Cup!

ENGLAND GAMES/GOALS
66/5

MILLIE BRIGHT
THE AERIAL THREAT!

WITH CAPTAIN Leah Williamson injured, England will look to Millie Bright to be a brick wall at the back. The towering defender sweeps up oppo attacks on the deck and clears everything in the air. She even bags plenty of goals at the other end!

DID YOU KNOW...

Mill has two dogs — a French bulldog called Zeus and a sausage dog called Hera!

HER TRADEMARK

MASSIVE HEADER!

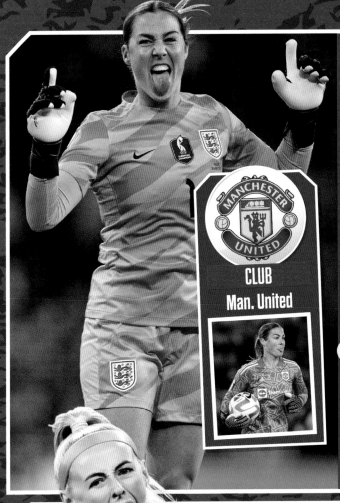

MARY EARPS

THE SUPER SHOT-STOPPER!

LIONESSES FANS SLEEP well at night knowing they've got a keeper as good as Mearps. She's England's undisputed first-choice keeper because of how good her shot-stopping tek is. She's the current FIFA Best Women's Goalkeeper after winning the award earlier this year!

CLUB
Man. United

AGE

30

POSITION
KEEPER

TOP MOMENT
Penalty saves in the Finalissima!

ENGLAND GAMES/GOALS
33/0

CHLOE KELLY

THE MAGIC MATCHWINNER!

CHLO KELL BROUGHT football home. Her extra-time finish won the Euros for England and her celebration was truly legendary. She's gone from strength to strength since then, dazzling defenders with her tricky wing play for club and country. She's super dangerous when she gets running!

CLUB
Man. City

AGE

25

POSITION
FORWARD

TOP MOMENT
Scoring the winner in the Euro 2022 final!

ENGLAND GAMES/GOALS
25/6

GEORGIA STANWAY

THE BOX-TO-BOX BALLER!

CLUB
Bayern Munich

DON'T SLEEP on Stanners — she's a true gamechanger. Georgia is a midfielder who's happy to battle with oppos for possession of the ball, picking up a few yellow cards along the way. Her defensive work is so important for England, but she's a top passer and has a wicked long shot on her, too!

AGE
24

POSITION
MIDFIELDER

TOP MOMENT
Long-range rocket v Spain!

ENGLAND GAMES/GOALS
49/15

LAUREN JAMES

THE BREAKOUT STAR!

CLUB
Chelsea

LOZ DIDN'T GO to the Euros in 2022, but she's exploded onto the scene ever since then, tearing it up in the WSL, terrorising defenders and ruining keepers' clean sheets. She's just starting her Lionesses career, but she's already showing the world how tekky her quick feet are!

AGE
21

POSITION
FORWARD

TOP MOMENT
First England goal
v South Korea!

ENGLAND GAMES/GOALS
10/1

CLUB
Barcelona

POSITION
MIDFIELDER

TOP MOMENT
Wicked assist in the Euro 2022 final!

ENGLAND GAMES/GOALS
58/0

KEIRA WALSH

THE PERFECT PASSER!

WALSH IS ONE of England's best players. She was named player of the match in the biggest game in Lioness history — the Euro 2022 final — thanks to her brilliance. She's one of the top playmakers in the world, capable of unlocking defences with one pinged through ball!

DID YOU KNOW...

Keira captained England when she was just 21 years old!

HER TRADEMARK

PIN-POINT THROUGH-BALLS!

21

BBC
MATCH OF THE DAY MAGAZINE

SHAW

JAMAICA

FACT FILE
Full name Khadija Monifa Shaw
Date of birth 31 January 1997 (age 26)
Place of birth Spanish Town, Jamaica
Position Striker Club Man. City

RAPINOE

U S A

FACT FILE

Full name Megan Anna Rapinoe
Date of birth 5 July 1985 (age 38)
Place of birth California, USA
Position Forward **Club** OL Reign

TOP 8
GOLDEN BOOT
CONTENDERS!

Meet the deadly goal machines who'll be battling it out to become the World Cup top scorer!

7

23 goals in 35 games for Spain

ESTHER GONZALEZ
SPAIN

CLUB: Real Madrid AGE: 30

THE SPANISH SENSATION has been the shining jewel in their front line, scoring and assisting from every angle. Esther's recent form at Real Madrid has made it seem like she scores goals in her sleep — she's not to be underestimated!

6

29 goals in 30 games for Nigeria

ASISAT OSHOALA
NIGERIA

CLUB: Barcelona AGE: 28

ASISAT HAS BEEN ELECTRIC for Barcelona, scoring almost 100 goals for them since joining in 2019. She's lightning quick and wicked in the air, making her a defender's nightmare. We can't wait to see her on the pitch this summer!

8

58 goals in 144 games for Netherlands

LIEKE MARTENS
NETHERLANDS

CLUB: PSG AGE: 30

LIEKE WAS NAMED World's Best Player in 2017, and her experience and quality make her a strong candidate for the Golden Boot. She did the business for Barcelona and now she's doing the same for PSG — she guarantees magic moments!

5

43 goals in 76 games for Norway

ADA HEGERBERG
NORWAY

CLUB: Lyon AGE: 27

THIS SUPERSTAR has broken more records than we've had hot dinners, and it doesn't look like Ada is stopping. She can play anywhere up front and is destined to score a worldie, so watch out for a some Hegerberg magic!

4

121 goals in 206 games for USA

ALEX MORGAN
USA

CLUB: San Diego Wave AGE: 33

ALEX WILL need to make some space in her trophy cabinet if she bags this one. Not only is she one of the best players in the women's game, but Alex has already won the World Cup twice and has three Golden Boots to her name!

3
LEA SCHULLER GERMANY

30 goals in 46 games for Germany

CLUB: Bayern Munich **AGE:** 25

THE BAYERN striker has provided goals galore for the Bundesliga leaders, and she's lethal at international level, too. Although Germany have a few strong contenders in the Golden Boot race, we reckon that Lea will be flying ahead of her rival teammates!

2
ALESSIA RUSSO ENGLAND

11 goals in 21 games for England

CLUB: Man. United **AGE:** 24

FROM SARINA WEIGMAN'S super sub to star striker, 'Less has been scoring goals for fun at club and country level. She was awesome for Man. United in 2022-23 and she'll be taking that sick form onto the biggest stage of all this summer!

1

AUSTRALIA

63 goals in 120 games for Australia

SAM KERR AUSTRALIA

CLUB: Chelsea **AGE:** 29

AS THE MATILDAS' record goalscorer, Sammy K is no stranger to winning the Golden Boot. In fact, she's the only female player to have won it in three different leagues, on three different continents. She's gonna be the one to beat this summer!

LIONESS FLASHBACK!

We've found some old photos of SEVEN ENGLAND STARS – but do you know who they are? Match them up!

ANSWERS ON p92!

1 +

2 +

3 +

4 +

5 +

6 +

7 +

A GREENWOOD

B HEMP

C KELLY

D WALSH

E DALY

F STANWAY

G TOONE

26

POPP

GERMANY

BBC
MATCH
OF THE DAY
MAGAZINE

FACT FILE

Full name Alexandra Pupp
Date of birth 6 April 1991 (age 32)
Place of birth Witten, Germany
Position Striker Club Wolfsburg

LOLS!

USA'S ALEX MORGAN IS...
TONGUE-OUT EMOJI

THE EMOJI MOVIE

WOMEN'S WORLD CUP EDITION!

ENGLAND'S MILLIE BRIGHT IS...
SUNGLASSES EMOJI

+

ENGLAND'S RACHEL DALY IS...
COWBOY HAT EMOJI

GERMANY'S ALEXANDRA POPP IS... HEAD BANDAGE EMOJI

JAMAICA'S KHADIJA SHAW IS... FACE-MASK EMOJI

DENMARK'S PERNILLE HARDER IS... SCARED-FACE EMOJI

SWEDEN'S LINA HURTIG IS... THINKING EMOJI

SPAIN'S ATHENEA DEL CASTILLO IS... GLASSES EMOJI

BRAZIL'S RAFAELLE SOUZA IS... SHUSHING EMOJI

29

BBC MATCH OF THE DAY MAGAZINE

THE UK'S BEST-SELLING FOOTY MAG!

If you love footy, then you'll love Match of the Day magazine!

+ Packed with the Prem's best ballers and global superstars!

+ Loaded with LOLs, quizzes, activities and epic posters!

+ Bursting with top skills advice, gaming tips and sick boot drops!

FUN-FILLED PAGES FOR YOUNG FOOTY FANS!

ON SALE EVERY FORTNIGHT!

No.1 MAG FOR WOMEN'S FOOTBALL!

And it tastes delicious!

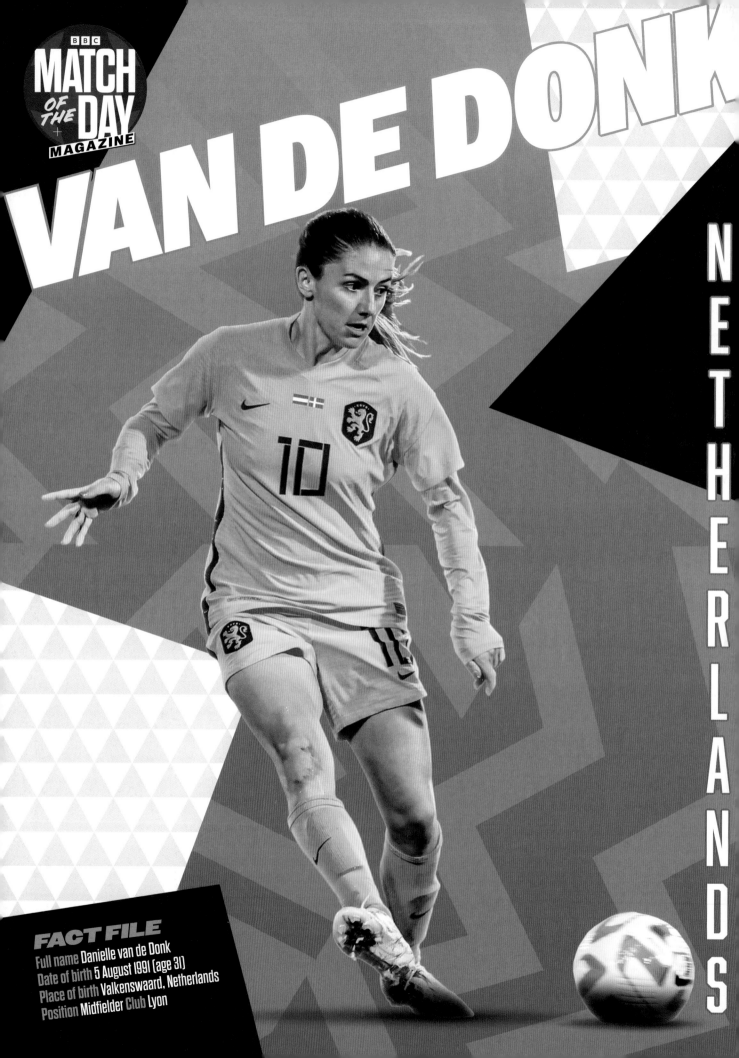

VAN DE DONK

NETHERLANDS

BBC MATCH OF THE DAY MAGAZINE

FACT FILE

Full name Danielle van de Donk
Date of birth 5 August 1991 (age 31)
Place of birth Valkenswaard, Netherlands
Position Midfielder Club Lyon

TRUE OR FALSE?

Some of these statements are true – CAN YOU WORK OUT WHICH ONES?

ANSWERS ON p92!

1

USA's legendary striker ALEX MORGAN is not just a danger on the pitch, she's a threat off it, too – she's a black belt in karate!

TRUE ✓ FALSE ✗

2

Since signing for Chelsea in 2020, Denmark captain PERNILLE HARDER has eaten fish, chips and mushy peas every single day!

TRUE ☐ FALSE ✗

3

England baller ELLA TOONE has got a pet koala that lives with her – she's named it Chloala Kelly after her Lioness team-mate!

TRUE ☐ FALSE ✗

4

Jamaica's striker KHADIJA SHAW, who plays for Man. City, is known as Bunny because as a kid she used to gobble up tons of carrots!

TRUE ✓ FALSE ✗

5

England star RACHEL DALY is a fully qualified doctor – she even helps out at her local hospital when they are short of staff!

TRUE ✓ FALSE ☐

33

REITEN

NORWAY

20 PLAYERS WHO WILL MAKE YOU SAY...

WOW!

SAM KERR

MOST LIKELY TO... **DO A BACKFLIP!**

This is the Australia striker's fourth World Cup — but having it in her own country makes it super special. The Chelsea star is one of the favourites for the Golden Boot so expect to see her trademark celebration!

AUSTRALIA

I SAW HER DO THIS! ✓

DELPHINE CASCARINO

FRANCE FFF

MOST LIKELY TO... *REMIND YOU OF MBAPPE!*

We're buzzing to see Lyon ace Delph in action. She's often compared to fellow France star Kylian Mbappe because of how she bursts into the box from wide, burns past defenders and fires off screamers. She's gonna do bits!

I SAW HER DO THIS! ✓

DEBINHA

MOST LIKELY TO... DANCE WITH DEFENDERS!

The Kansas City star has so much talent. We love seeing her bring Brazil's samba swagger to the biggest games, too. Like the best South American ballers, the forward loves to pull off a nutmeg, a flick or a scoop to change the game!

CBF

I SAW HER DO THIS!

KEIRA WALSH

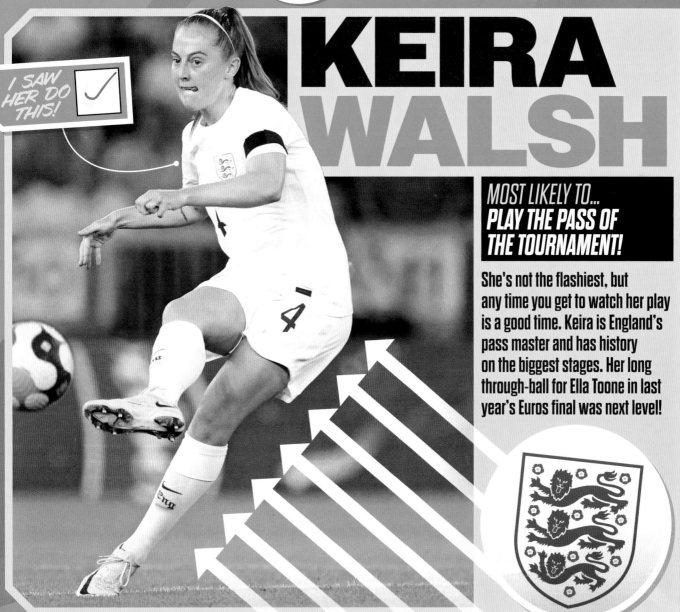

I SAW HER DO THIS!

MOST LIKELY TO... PLAY THE PASS OF THE TOURNAMENT!

She's not the flashiest, but any time you get to watch her play is a good time. Keira is England's pass master and has history on the biggest stages. Her long through-ball for Ella Toone in last year's Euros final was next level!

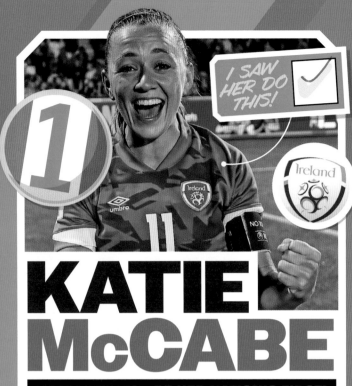

①

KATIE McCABE

I SAW HER DO THIS! ✓

MOST LIKELY TO... *BE HER NATION'S FIRST!*

Republic Of Ireland have never been to the World Cup before, so it could be tough for them. If anyone's going to write their name into the history books and score their first World Cup goal, it'll be this all-action winger!

JI SO-YUN

I SAW HER DO THIS! ✓

MOST LIKELY TO... *BE THE ONE-TOUCH QUEEN!*

WSL fans know what Ji is capable of. In her time at Chelsea, the South Korea star's one-touch tek helped them win trophies — and her skills will be key for her country. She only needs one moment to change a game!

ALEXIA PUTELLAS

I SAW HER DO THIS! ✓

MOST LIKELY TO... *BE THE BEST AT EVERYTHING!*

There's a reason why Lexi has won the Ballon d'Or two years in a row — she's incredible at everything. The Spain star always does something that gets people out of their seats, from scoring a goal out of nowhere to creating a goalscoring chance with an elite pass!

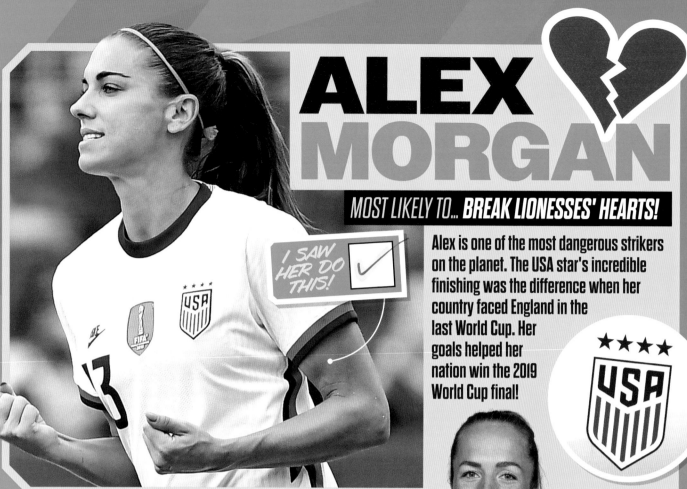

ALEX MORGAN

MOST LIKELY TO... **BREAK LIONESSES' HEARTS!**

I SAW HER DO THIS! ✓

Alex is one of the most dangerous strikers on the planet. The USA star's incredible finishing was the difference when her country faced England in the last World Cup. Her goals helped her nation win the 2019 World Cup final!

I SAW HER DO THIS! ✓

FRIDOLINA ROLFO

MOST LIKELY TO... **SCORE WITH A ROCKET!**

Frido's highlights reel for Sweden is packed full of left-foot finishes. She smashes in delicious volleys, placed strikes and clinical one-on-ones — but the Barcelona star loves scoring long-range bangers with her left peg!

I SAW HER DO THIS! ✓

LIA WALTI

MOST LIKELY TO... **SMILE THROUGH IT ALL!**

The Arsenal and Switzerland midfielder is a real battler. The two-footed technician will put in an epic shift for her team and, on top of everything, she always plays with a huge smile on her face. You love to see it!

LINETH BEERENSTEYN

I SAW HER DO THIS! ✓

MOST LIKELY TO... *BE TOO FAST TO HANDLE!*

Speed is so important, which makes Juventus forward Lineth a key player for the Netherlands. Her rapid, explosive dribbling causes defenders nightmares when she's steaming at them on the counter-attack!

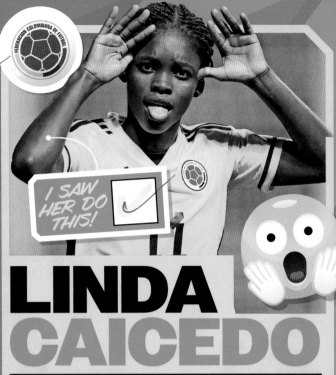

LINDA CAICEDO

I SAW HER DO THIS! ✓

MOST LIKELY TO... *SHOCK THE WORLD!*

Colombia skiller Caicedo is only 18, but the Real Madrid wonderkid is one of the most exciting players around. The World Cup is the perfect stage for Linda to show off her dribbling, vision and flair!

PERNILLE HARDER

MOST LIKELY TO... *INSPIRE A NATION!*

The Denmark star is a great finisher and top creator but we're most buzzing to see how she gets her country up for the fight. She inspires everyone with her work-rate and on-pitch presence. She'll give everything for the win!

I SAW HER DO THIS! ✓

YUI HASEGAWA

MOST LIKELY TO... **MAKE A DEFENDER RETIRE!**

Some of the tricks Yui pulls off are RUDE. Japan's classy Man. City midfielder drifts around the pitch using her incredible first touch to pop the ball over a defender's head before playing a ridiculous pass. She makes the oppo look silly!

I SAW HER DO THIS!

JAPAN JFA

I SAW HER DO THIS!

HAITI

MELCHIE DUMORNAY

MOST LIKELY TO... **CAUSE A HUGE UPSET!**

Melchie is one of the flamiest young stars. She's scored eight times in 12 games for Haiti, including the injury-time goal that helped them qualify for their first World Cup. Her tek could create history this summer!

I SAW HER DO THIS!

NIGERIA FOOTBALL FEDERATION 1945

ASISAT OSHOALA

MOST LIKELY TO... **DOMINATE IN THE BOX!**

Barcelona's prolific Nigerian striker is maybe the best female African baller ever. She finishes everything that drops her way, using her speed strength and height to devastate defenders!

CHRISTINE SINCLAIR

MOST LIKELY TO... **ROLL BACK THE YEARS!**

Christine has scored more goals for Canada than some players play games in their career. The 39-year-old striker has scored 190 times for her country and we just know she'll be bagging again at potentially her last major tournament!

I SAW HER DO THIS! ✓

CANADA®

SINCLAIR, 🍁 COULD I HAVE THE 👕 OF THE BEST STRIKER?

CAROLINE GRAHAM HANSEN

NORGE

I SAW HER DO THIS! ✓

MOST LIKELY TO... **SKIN HER DEFENDER!**

Norway have some truly elite talents in their squad, but we can't wait to see this Barcelona dynamo teach defenders some lessons. Hansen flies past oppos with ease, setting up chances for Ada Hegerberg or netting a wonder goal herself!

ALEXANDRA POPP

MOST LIKELY TO... SCORE A HAT-TRICK!

Morocco and Colombia could be in for a tough time in the group stage — they'll face a Germany striker who wants revenge. Popp is going to be hunting for all the goals she can find after her country's defeat by England in the Euro 2022 final!

I SAW HER DO THIS!

KHADIJA SHAW

MOST LIKELY TO... BE UNSTOPPABLE IN THE AIR!

Bunny has been in red-hot form since joining Man. City, scoring all kinds of goals — but she's deadly with her head, bagging six in the WSL alone this season. We reckon she'll be adding to her 31 Jamaica goals through a bullet header!

I SAW HER DO THIS!

43

PERISSET

FRANCE

Eve Josette Noelle Perisset
24 December 1994 (age 28)
Saint Priest, France
Full-back   Chelsea

BLACKSTENIUS

SWEDEN

FACT FILE
Full name Emma Stina Blackstenius
Date of birth 5 February 1996 (age 27)
Place of birth Vadstena, Sweden
Position Striker Club Arsenal

LIONESSES

It's time to test your knowledge of THE ENGLAND SQUAD!

ANSWERS ON p92!

1

WHO'S CELEBRATING WITH CHLOE KELLY HERE?

| A Alex Greenwood | ✓ | B Beth England | |
| C Ella Toone | | D Leah Williamson | |

2

WHICH IS OF THESE IS THE CORRECT ENGLAND WOMEN'S BADGE?

A ☐   B ☐   C ✓   D ☐

3

WHO IS HIDING IN THIS PIC?

A Millie Bright ☐

B Keira Walsh ☐

C Beth Mead ☐

D Georgia Stanway ✓

4

WHICH PUNDIT IS EX-LIONESS JILL SCOTT?

A   B ✓

C ✗   D

5

WHICH OF THESE TROPHIES DID ENGLAND WIN IN 2022?

A   B

C   D ✓

QUIZ!

6 WHICH CLUB DOES ENGLAND KEEPER MARY EARPS PLAY FOR?

- A Arsenal
- B Barcelona
- C Man. United ✓
- D Man. City

7 THESE FOUR ENGLAND LIONESSES ALL PLAY IN WHICH POSITION?

 Rachel Daly Alessia Russo  Lauren James  Chloe Kelly

- A Keeper
- B Centre-back
- C Midfielder
- D Forward ✓

8

WHAT IS LUCY BRONZE'S MIDDLE NAME?

- A Tough ✓
- B Strong
- C Solid
- D Power

9 WHICH COUNTRY DOES ENGLAND BOSS SARINA WIEGMAN COME FROM?

- A Austria
- B Netherlands ✓
- C Switzerland
- D Sweden

10 WHICH OF THESE IS THE ENGLAND AWAY KIT?

 A
 B
 C
 D ✓

MY LIONESS LEVEL!

TURN TO PAGE 92 FOR THE ANSWERS, THEN GRADE HOW MUCH YOU KNOW ABOUT ENGLAND!

10	ROAR WITH PRIDE
8	TIGER
6	LEOPARD
4	WILD CAT
2	DOMESTIC CAT
0	KITTEN

YOUR SCORE ☐ /10

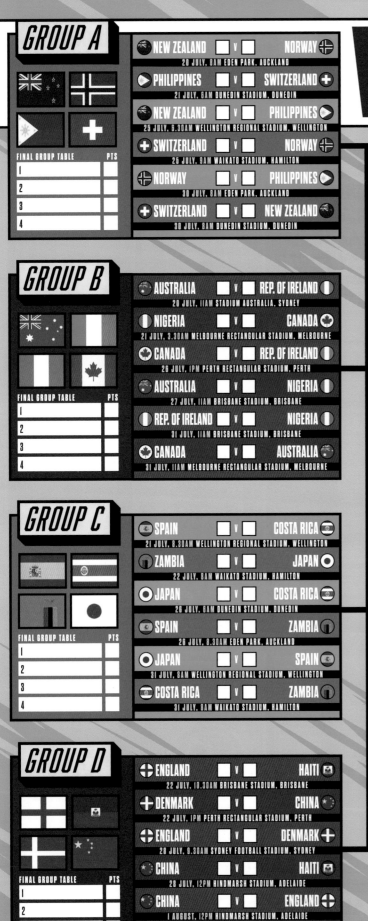

GROUP A

NEW ZEALAND	☐	v	☐	NORWAY	
20 JULY, 8AM EDEN PARK, AUCKLAND					
PHILIPPINES	☐	v	☐	SWITZERLAND	
21 JULY, 6AM DUNEDIN STADIUM, DUNEDIN					
NEW ZEALAND	☐	v	☐	PHILIPPINES	
25 JULY, 6.30AM WELLINGTON REGIONAL STADIUM, WELLINGTON					
SWITZERLAND	☐	v	☐	NORWAY	
25 JULY, 9AM WAIKATO STADIUM, HAMILTON					
NORWAY	☐	v	☐	PHILIPPINES	
30 JULY, 8AM EDEN PARK, AUCKLAND					
SWITZERLAND	☐	v	☐	NEW ZEALAND	
30 JULY, 6AM DUNEDIN STADIUM, DUNEDIN					

FINAL GROUP TABLE	PTS
1	
2	
3	
4	

GROUP B

AUSTRALIA	☐	v	☐	REP. OF IRELAND	
20 JULY, 11AM STADIUM AUSTRALIA, SYDNEY					
NIGERIA	☐	v	☐	CANADA	
21 JULY, 3.30AM MELBOURNE RECTANGULAR STADIUM, MELBOURNE					
CANADA	☐	v	☐	REP. OF IRELAND	
26 JULY, 1PM PERTH RECTANGULAR STADIUM, PERTH					
AUSTRALIA	☐	v	☐	NIGERIA	
27 JULY, 11AM BRISBANE STADIUM, BRISBANE					
REP. OF IRELAND	☐	v	☐	NIGERIA	
31 JULY, 11AM BRISBANE STADIUM, BRISBANE					
CANADA	☐	v	☐	AUSTRALIA	
31 JULY, 11AM MELBOURNE RECTANGULAR STADIUM, MELBOURNE					

FINAL GROUP TABLE	PTS
1	
2	
3	
4	

GROUP C

SPAIN	☐	v	☐	COSTA RICA	
21 JULY, 8.30AM WELLINGTON REGIONAL STADIUM, WELLINGTON					
ZAMBIA	☐	v	☐	JAPAN	
22 JULY, 6AM WAIKATO STADIUM, HAMILTON					
JAPAN	☐	v	☐	COSTA RICA	
26 JULY, 6AM DUNEDIN STADIUM, DUNEDIN					
SPAIN	☐	v	☐	ZAMBIA	
26 JULY, 8.30AM EDEN PARK, AUCKLAND					
JAPAN	☐	v	☐	SPAIN	
31 JULY, 6AM WELLINGTON REGIONAL STADIUM, WELLINGTON					
COSTA RICA	☐	v	☐	ZAMBIA	
31 JULY, 6AM WAIKATO STADIUM, HAMILTON					

FINAL GROUP TABLE	PTS
1	
2	
3	
4	

GROUP D

ENGLAND	☐	v	☐	HAITI	
22 JULY, 10.30AM BRISBANE STADIUM, BRISBANE					
DENMARK	☐	v	☐	CHINA	
22 JULY, 1PM PERTH RECTANGULAR STADIUM, PERTH					
ENGLAND	☐	v	☐	DENMARK	
28 JULY, 9.30AM SYDNEY FOOTBALL STADIUM, SYDNEY					
CHINA	☐	v	☐	HAITI	
28 JULY, 12PM HINDMARSH STADIUM, ADELAIDE					
CHINA	☐	v	☐	ENGLAND	
1 AUGUST, 12PM HINDMARSH STADIUM, ADELAIDE					
HAITI	☐	v	☐	DENMARK	
1 AUGUST, 12PM PERTH RECTANGULAR STADIUM, PERTH					

FINAL GROUP TABLE	PTS
1	
2	
3	
4	

WORLD CU

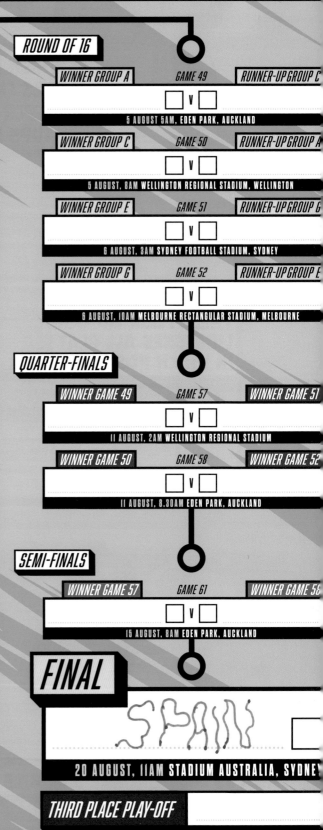

ROUND OF 16

WINNER GROUP A	GAME 49	RUNNER-UP GROUP C
☐ v ☐		
5 AUGUST 5AM, EDEN PARK, AUCKLAND		

WINNER GROUP C	GAME 50	RUNNER-UP GROUP A
☐ v ☐		
5 AUGUST, 8AM WELLINGTON REGIONAL STADIUM, WELLINGTON		

WINNER GROUP E	GAME 51	RUNNER-UP GROUP G
☐ v ☐		
6 AUGUST, 3AM SYDNEY FOOTBALL STADIUM, SYDNEY		

WINNER GROUP G	GAME 52	RUNNER-UP GROUP E
☐ v ☐		
6 AUGUST, 10AM MELBOURNE RECTANGULAR STADIUM, MELBOURNE		

QUARTER-FINALS

WINNER GAME 49	GAME 57	WINNER GAME 51
☐ v ☐		
11 AUGUST, 2AM WELLINGTON REGIONAL STADIUM		

WINNER GAME 50	GAME 58	WINNER GAME 52
☐ v ☐		
11 AUGUST, 8.30AM EDEN PARK, AUCKLAND		

SEMI-FINALS

WINNER GAME 57	GAME 61	WINNER GAME 58
☐ v ☐		
15 AUGUST, 8AM EDEN PARK, AUCKLAND		

FINAL

SPAIN

20 AUGUST, 11AM STADIUM AUSTRALIA, SYDNEY

THIRD PLACE PLAY-OFF

2023

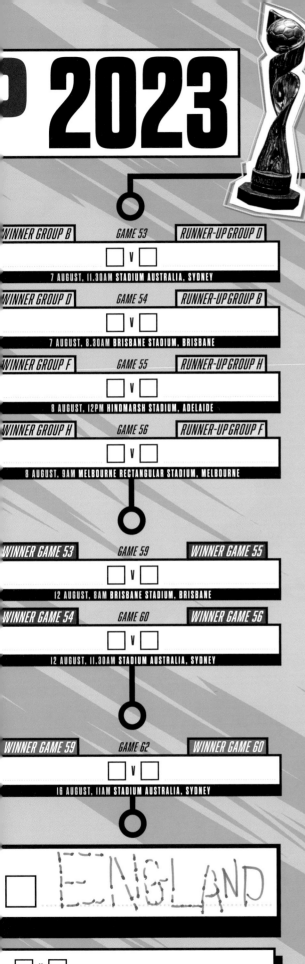

WINNER GROUP B — GAME 53 — **RUNNER-UP GROUP D**
☐ v ☐
7 AUGUST, 11.30AM STADIUM AUSTRALIA, SYDNEY

WINNER GROUP D — GAME 54 — **RUNNER-UP GROUP B**
☐ v ☐
7 AUGUST, 8.30AM BRISBANE STADIUM, BRISBANE

WINNER GROUP F — GAME 55 — **RUNNER-UP GROUP H**
☐ v ☐
8 AUGUST, 12PM HINDMARSH STADIUM, ADELAIDE

WINNER GROUP H — GAME 56 — **RUNNER-UP GROUP F**
☐ v ☐
8 AUGUST, 9AM MELBOURNE RECTANGULAR STADIUM, MELBOURNE

WINNER GAME 53 — GAME 59 — **WINNER GAME 55**
☐ v ☐
12 AUGUST, 8AM BRISBANE STADIUM, BRISBANE

WINNER GAME 54 — GAME 60 — **WINNER GAME 56**
☐ v ☐
12 AUGUST, 11.30AM STADIUM AUSTRALIA, SYDNEY

WINNER GAME 59 — GAME 62 — **WINNER GAME 60**
☐ v ☐
16 AUGUST, 11AM STADIUM AUSTRALIA, SYDNEY

☐ ENGLAND

☐ v ☐
19 AUGUST, 9AM BRISBANE STADIUM, BRISBANE

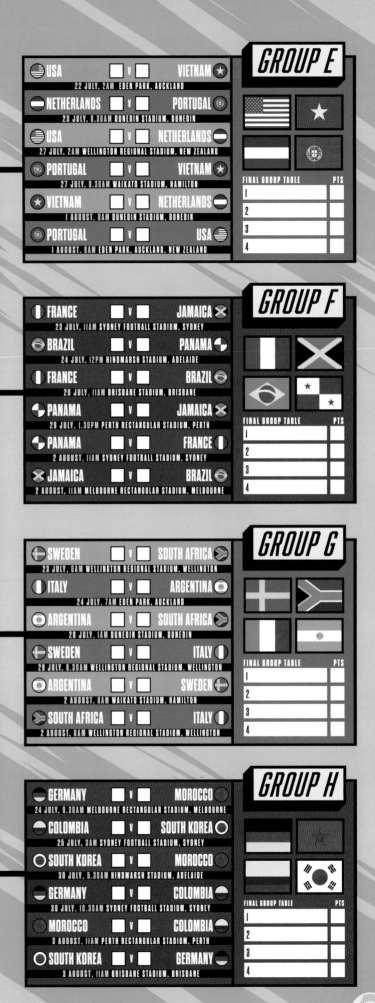

GROUP E

USA ☐ v ☐ VIETNAM
22 JULY, 2AM EDEN PARK, AUCKLAND

NETHERLANDS ☐ v ☐ PORTUGAL
23 JULY, 8.30AM DUNEDIN STADIUM, DUNEDIN

USA ☐ v ☐ NETHERLANDS
27 JULY, 2AM WELLINGTON REGIONAL STADIUM, NEW ZEALAND

PORTUGAL ☐ v ☐ VIETNAM
27 JULY, 8.30AM WAIKATO STADIUM, HAMILTON

VIETNAM ☐ v ☐ NETHERLANDS
1 AUGUST, 8AM DUNEDIN STADIUM, DUNEDIN

PORTUGAL ☐ v ☐ USA
1 AUGUST, 8AM EDEN PARK, AUCKLAND, NEW ZEALAND

FINAL GROUP TABLE	PTS
1	
2	
3	
4	

GROUP F

FRANCE ☐ v ☐ JAMAICA
23 JULY, 11AM SYDNEY FOOTBALL STADIUM, SYDNEY

BRAZIL ☐ v ☐ PANAMA
24 JULY, 12PM HINDMARSH STADIUM, ADELAIDE

FRANCE ☐ v ☐ BRAZIL
29 JULY, 11AM BRISBANE STADIUM, BRISBANE

PANAMA ☐ v ☐ JAMAICA
29 JULY, 1.30PM PERTH RECTANGULAR STADIUM, PERTH

PANAMA ☐ v ☐ FRANCE
2 AUGUST, 11AM SYDNEY FOOTBALL STADIUM, SYDNEY

JAMAICA ☐ v ☐ BRAZIL
2 AUGUST, 11AM MELBOURNE RECTANGULAR STADIUM, MELBOURNE

FINAL GROUP TABLE	PTS
1	
2	
3	
4	

GROUP G

SWEDEN ☐ v ☐ SOUTH AFRICA
23 JULY, 6AM WELLINGTON REGIONAL STADIUM, WELLINGTON

ITALY ☐ v ☐ ARGENTINA
24 JULY, 7AM EDEN PARK, AUCKLAND

ARGENTINA ☐ v ☐ SOUTH AFRICA
28 JULY, 1AM DUNEDIN STADIUM, DUNEDIN

SWEDEN ☐ v ☐ ITALY
29 JULY, 6.30AM WELLINGTON REGIONAL STADIUM, WELLINGTON

ARGENTINA ☐ v ☐ SWEDEN
2 AUGUST, 8AM WAIKATO STADIUM, HAMILTON

SOUTH AFRICA ☐ v ☐ ITALY
2 AUGUST, 8AM WELLINGTON REGIONAL STADIUM, WELLINGTON

FINAL GROUP TABLE	PTS
1	
2	
3	
4	

GROUP H

GERMANY ☐ v ☐ MOROCCO
24 JULY, 8.30AM MELBOURNE RECTANGULAR STADIUM, MELBOURNE

COLOMBIA ☐ v ☐ SOUTH KOREA
25 JULY, 3AM SYDNEY FOOTBALL STADIUM, SYDNEY

SOUTH KOREA ☐ v ☐ MOROCCO
30 JULY, 5.30AM HINDMARSH STADIUM, ADELAIDE

GERMANY ☐ v ☐ COLOMBIA
30 JULY, 10.30AM SYDNEY FOOTBALL STADIUM, SYDNEY

MOROCCO ☐ v ☐ COLOMBIA
3 AUGUST, 11AM PERTH RECTANGULAR STADIUM, PERTH

SOUTH KOREA ☐ v ☐ GERMANY
3 AUGUST, 11AM BRISBANE STADIUM, BRISBANE

FINAL GROUP TABLE	PTS
1	
2	
3	
4	

49

HARDER

DENMARK

FACT FILE
Full name Pernille Mosegaard Harder
Date of birth 15 November 1992 (age 30)
Place of birth Ikast, Denmark
Position Midfielder

THE ULTIMATE
WORLD CUP
GROUP GUIDE!

THE STAR PLAYERS / THE LINE-UPS / THE TACTICS / THE RATINGS

NORWAY

FACT FILE

Nickname: The Grasshoppers
Manager: Hege Riise
Captain: Maren Mjelde
WWC qualifying: Group F winners
FIFA ranking: 13

WORLD CUP RECORD
BEST RESULT
Champions (1995)

IF THEY WERE AN ANIMAL, THEY'D BE...

A MOOSE!
Cool, calm and can overpower most — but can be startled by strong opposition!

NORWAY FACTS
Greatest ever player: Ada Hegerberg
Current league champions: Brann
Language: Norwegian
Population: 5.4 million **Capital:** Oslo

FORM	★★★★☆
EXPERIENCE	★★★★☆
DEFENCE	★★★★☆
ATTACK	★★★★★
OVERALL	★★★★☆

STAR PLAYER
GURO REITEN
Club: Chelsea
Position: Midfielder
Age: 28

STRONGEST LINE-UP!

MIKALSEN

T. HANSEN · MJELDE · BERGSVAND · LUND

MAANUM · ENGEN

EIKELAND · C. HANSEN · REITEN

HEGERBEG

FORMATION 4-2-3-1 PLAYING STYLE PATIENT

✔ STRENGTHS

Norway have a solid midfield with WSL stars Frida Maanum and Guro Reiten. They also have the goalscoring superpower of former World Player of the Year Ada Hegerberg!

✗ WEAKNESSES

Despite some strong results, when Norway's rhythm is broken, they find it hard to recover. They've got clever passes and a great vision, but they lack pace and a tight defence!

VERDICT The 1995 World Cup winners haven't made the final four for 16 years but they've got a blend of experienced players and fresh talent. One to watch!

THE REST OF
✛ GROUP A ✛

Hannah Wilkinson

🇳🇿 NEW ZEALAND

Formation: 4-4-2 **Playing style:** Counter-attacking
Strengths: Some strong defenders who are versatile enough to play in midfield!
Weaknesses: The squad lacks experience at the highest levels, which could cost them!
Star player: Hannah Wilkinson, Melbourne City

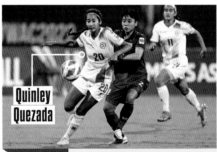

Quinley Quezada

PHILIPPINES

Formation: 4-4-2 **Playing style:** Counter-attacking
Strengths: Experienced coach Alen Stajcic has the tactical know-how to get results!
Weaknesses: As this is their first World Cup, the big stage might be too much for these newbies!
Star player: Quinley Quezada, Red Star Belgrade

Lia Walti

✛ SWITZERLAND

Formation: 4-2-3-1 **Playing style:** Defensive
Strengths: A squad full of European club talent playing in some of the best leagues!
Weaknesses: The midfield is solid, but this team will struggle against strong opposition!
Star player: Lia Walti, Arsenal

AUSTRALIA

FACT FILE

Nickname: The Matildas
Manager: Tony Gustavsson
Captain: Sam Kerr
WWC qualifying: Co-hosts.
FIFA ranking: 12

STAR PLAYER

SAM KERR
Club: Chelsea
Position: Striker
Age: 29

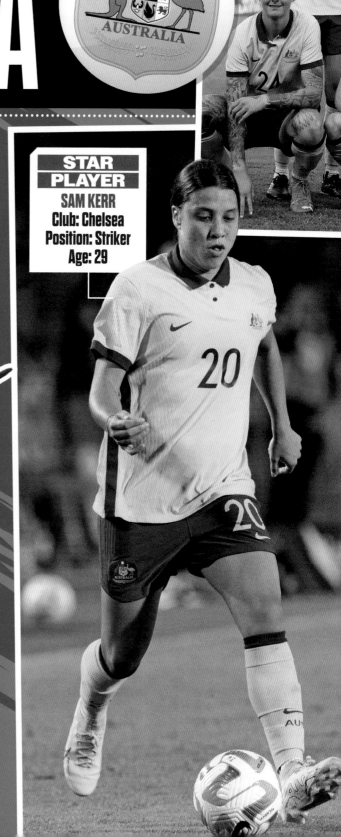

WORLD CUP RECORD

BEST RESULT
Quarter-finals
(2007, 2011, 2015)

IF THEY WERE AN ANIMAL, THEY'D BE...

A KANGAROO!

Will have a spring in their step on home soil.
Could hop, skip and jump out of the groups!

AUSTRALIA FACTS

Greatest ever player: Sam Kerr
Current league champions: Sydney FC
Language: English
Population: 25.6m **Capital:** Canberra

FORM	★★★★☆
EXPERIENCE	★★★☆☆
DEFENCE	★★★½☆
ATTACK	★★★★☆
OVERALL	★★★★☆

STRONGEST LINE-UP!

ARNOLD

GRANT   **POLINGHORNE**   **KENNEDY**   **CATLEY**

GORRY   **COONEY-CROSS**

VINE   **FOORD**   **RASO**

KERR

FORMATION 4-2-3-1 PLAYING STYLE DEFENSIVE

✔ STRENGTHS

No doubt about it, the Matildas have got some top-quality players in their squad — and any team with Sam Kerr starting up front will fancy their chances of finding the back of the net!

✗ WEAKNESSES

While their form has been strong, the Aussies have struggled when they've come up against tough opposition — the likes of Spain and Canada have exposed some big gaps in their defence!

VERDICT An ace line-up with some WSL stars who will be hungry for goals, and while on home soil, they could be one of the nations to watch!

THE REST OF ✛ GROUP B ✛

Christine Sinclair

🍁 CANADA

Formation: 4-2-3-1 Playing style: Patient
Strengths: Canada have bags of experience. Christine Sinclair has over 300 caps and nearly 200 goals!
Weaknesses: The USA. Canada have only beaten them four times in their history!
Star player: Christine Sinclair, Portland Thorns

Katie McCabe

REP. OF IRELAND

Formation: 5-4-1 Playing style: Defensive
Strengths: Most of their goals come from top midfielders, Katie McCabe and Denise O'Sullivan!
Weaknesses: They've got a stacked squad full of WSL ballers, but they fall short against tough opponents!
Star player: Katie McCabe, Arsenal

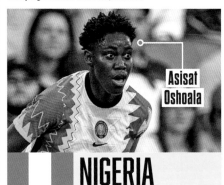

Asisat Oshoala

NIGERIA

Formation: 4-3-3 Playing style: Pressing
Strengths: The squad has some elite players, such as Barcelona's Asisat Oshoala and Seville's Toni Payne!
Weaknesses: Experience. Nigeria aren't dominant, and their defence has been stretched at times!
Star player: Asisat Oshoala, Barcelona

SPAIN

FACT FILE

Nickname: La Roja (The Reds)
Manager: Jorge Vilda
Captain: Jennifer Hermoso
WWC qualifying: Group B winners
FIFA ranking: 7

WORLD CUP RECORD

BEST RESULT
Round of 16 (2019)

IF THEY WERE AN ANIMAL, THEY'D BE...

A TIGER!
Pacy, punchy and passionate, they expect to get their paws on the prize!

SPAIN FACTS
Greatest ever player: Alexia Putellas
Current league champions: Barcelona
Language: Spanish
Population: 47.4m **Capital:** Madrid

FORM	★★★★☆
EXPERIENCE	★★★★☆
DEFENCE	★★★½☆
ATTACK	★★★★★
OVERALL	★★★★☆

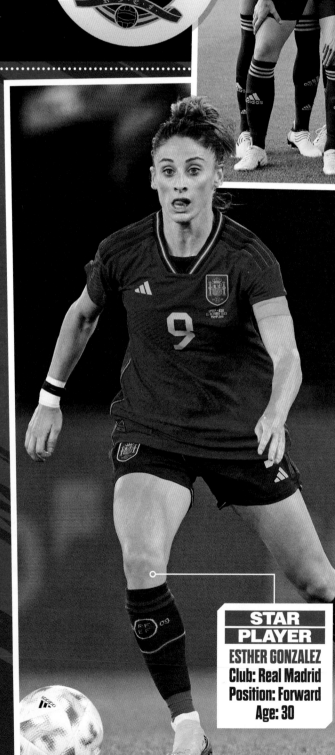

STAR PLAYER
ESTHER GONZALEZ
Club: Real Madrid
Position: Forward
Age: 30

STRONGEST LINE-UP!

RODRIGUEZ

GARCIA PAREDES ANDRES CARMONA

OROZ ABELLEIRA

MARTINEZ HERMOSO CASTILLO

GONZALEZ

FORMATION 4-2-3-1 PLAYING STYLE PASSING

✔ STRENGTHS

A talented team of pass-and-move ballers, who have mostly come from Barcelona and Real Madrid. They're quick, dynamic and creative!

✘ WEAKNESSES

Unfortunately, due to a dispute with Spanish football chiefs and the manager, a number of their best 11 have withdrawn from the squad!

VERDICT Despite some big-name squad drop-outs, Spain will bring bags of talent to the World Cup this summer — watch out for their ballin' tek!

THE REST OF
✛ GROUP C ✛

Raquel Rodriguez

COSTA RICA

Formation: 3-4-3 Playing style: Defensive
Strengths: Some top young talent emerging from this squad, including Glasgow City's Priscila Chinchilla!
Weaknesses: Not being clinical enough in front of goal and lacking a solid defence!
Star player: Raquel Rodriguez, Portland Thorns

Mana Iwabuchi

JAPAN

Formation: 4-4-2 Playing style: Counter-attacking
Strengths: They've got talent, pace and creativity, and have beaten Brazil and drawn against USA!
Weaknesses: The squad is short on players with serious big-league experience!
Star player: Mana Iwabuchi, Arsenal

Barbra Banda

ZAMBIA

Formation: 4-4-2 Playing style: Counter-attacking
Strengths: Some pacy forwards and young talent emerging in the Spanish second division!
Weaknesses: Their first World Cup might be daunting for some of the less experienced players!
Star player: Barbra Banda, Shanghai Shengli

ENGLAND

FACT FILE

Nickname: The Lionesses
Manager: Sarina Wiegman
Captain: Leah Williamson
WWC qualifying: Group D winners
FIFA ranking: 4

WORLD CUP RECORD

BEST RESULT
Third place (2015)

IF THEY WERE AN ANIMAL, THEY'D BE...

A LIONESS!
Classy, powerful and totally roarsome. After tasting success, they're hungry for more!

ENGLAND FACTS
Greatest ever player: Ellen White
Current league champions: Chelsea
Language: English
Population: 55.98m **Capital:** London

FORM	★★★★★
EXPERIENCE	★★★★★
DEFENCE	★★★★★
ATTACK	★★★★★
OVERALL	★★★★★

STAR PLAYER

LUCY BRONZE
Club: Barcelona
Position: Right-back
Age: 31

THE REST OF
✛ GROUP D ✛

Wang Shuang

CHINA

Formation: 4-4-2 **Playing style:** Counter-attacking
Strengths: An experienced team in big tournaments, they dominate in the Women's Asian Cup!
Weaknesses: China have really struggled for goals recently — which is a big concern!
Star player: Wang Shuang, Racing Louisville

Pernille Harder

✛ DENMARK

Formation: 3-4-3 **Playing style:** Defensive
Strengths: Some fresh faces, like Arsenal's Kathrine Kuhl, is paired with plenty of experienced players.
Weaknesses: Denmark's defence isn't the strongest and they concede goals far too easily!
Star player: Pernille Harder

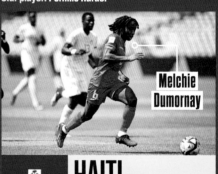

Melchie Dumornay

HAITI

Formation: 4-2-3-1 **Playing style:** Defensive
Strengths: Nerilia Mondesir has bagged an incredible 18 goals in just ten games!
Weaknesses: A weak defence and not enough creative play to get past top teams!
Star player: Melchie Dumornay, Reims

STRONGEST LINE-UP!

EARPS

BRONZE · BRIGHT · GREENWOOD · DALY

STANWAY · WALSH · TOONE

JAMES · RUSSO · HEMP

FORMATION 4-3-3 PLAYING STYLE PRESSING

✔ STRENGTHS

Sarina Wiegman has turned the Lionesses into big-time winners. They're the total package — from one of the world's best in goal to a deadly frontline!

✗ WEAKNESSES

Two of their biggest heroes from their Euro 2022 triumph, Leah Williamson and Beth Mead, are both recovering from major injuries — they'd be a huge loss for any team!

VERDICT A team in tip-top form and with plenty of world-class ballers. England will be tough to beat at the finals!

USA

FACT FILE

Nickname: The Stars and Stripes
Manager: Vlatko Andonovski
Captain: Becky Sauerbrunn
WWC qualifying: CONCACAF Group A winners **FIFA ranking:** 1

WORLD CUP RECORD

BEST RESULT
Champions (1991, 1999, 2015, 2019)

IF THEY WERE AN ANIMAL, THEY'D BE...

AN EAGLE!
Top of the food chain, they'll dismantle their prey once they get their claws into them!

USA FACTS
Greatest ever player: Abby Wambach
Current league champions: OL Reign
Language: English **Population:** 331.9m
Capital: Washington D.C

FORM	★★★★★
EXPERIENCE	★★★★★
DEFENCE	★★★★☆
ATTACK	★★★★⯪
OVERALL	★★★★⯪

STAR PLAYER
ALEX MORGAN
Club: San Diego Wave
Position: Striker
Age: 33

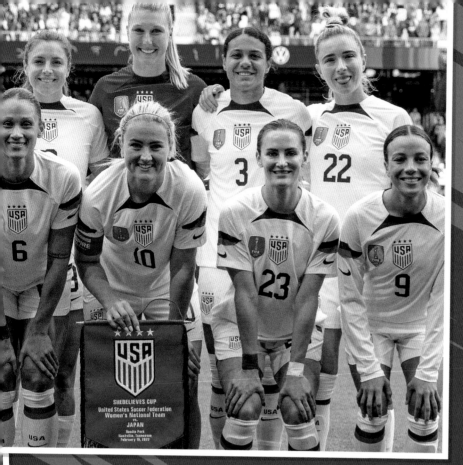

THE REST OF +GROUP E+

Danielle van de Donk

NETHERLANDS

Formation: 4-3-3 **Playing style:** Creative and attacking
Strengths: A squad packed with quality from some of Europe's biggest clubs!
Weaknesses: Losing Vivianne Miedema will make goalscoring much harder!
Star player: Danielle van de Donk, Lyon

Dolores Silva

PORTUGAL

Formation: 4-3-3 **Playing style:** Counter-attacking
Strengths: Loads of pace in midfield and wingers who play high and wide!
Weaknesses: This Portugal team can find both creating and scoring goals a problem!
Star player: Dolores Silva, Braga

Huynh Nhu

VIETNAM

Formation: 4-4-2 **Playing style:** Counter-attacking
Strengths: Nguyen Thi Tuyet Dung has great vision and plays clever passes. She's one to watch!
Weaknesses: Their players lack experience outside of the Vietnamese domestic league!
Star player: Huynh Nhu, Lank Vilaverdense

STRONGEST LINE-UP!

NAEHER

FOX · COOK · SAUERBRUNN · DUNN

HORAN · SULLIVAN · LAVELLE

RODMAN · MORGAN · SMITH

FORMATION 4-3-3 PLAYING STYLE PRESSING

✔ STRENGTHS

The USA collect silverware like stars on their flag and have won the most titles in tournament history. With bags of new talent paired with experience, this team know how to win on the biggest stage!

✗ WEAKNESSES

This team definitely know how to win, but their midfield has struggled in recent matches against England and Spain. Their passing needs to be sharper if they want to dominate in midfield!

VERDICT This talented USA team are desperate to make it five World Cup wins at this tournament. But with so many good teams around, it won't be easy!

BRAZIL

FACT FILE

Nickname: Selecao
Manager: Pia Sundhage
Captain: Marta
WWC qualifying: Copa America winners
FIFA ranking: 9

STAR PLAYER

DEBINHA
Club: Kansas City
Position: Forward
Age: 31

WORLD CUP RECORD

BEST RESULT

Runners-up (2007)

IF THEY WERE AN ANIMAL, THEY'D BE...

A JAGUAR!

Iconic colouring, smart and skilful — these cool cats can be impossible to stop!

BRAZIL FACTS

Greatest ever player: Formiga
Current league champions: Palmeiras
Language: Portuguese
Population: 214.3m **Capital:** Brasilia

FORM	★★★★☆
EXPERIENCE	★★★★☆
DEFENCE	★★★½☆
ATTACK	★★★½☆
OVERALL	★★★★☆

STRONGEST LINE-UP!

IZIDORO

LAUREN   KATHELLEN   RAFAELLE

ANTONIA   TAMIRES

BORGES   LUANA   KEROLIN

BEATRIZ   GEYSE

FORMATION 5-3-2 PLAYING STYLE POSSESSION

✓ STRENGTHS

These Brazilian ballers have got bags of experience in some of the world's top leagues. They've got loads of talent in attacking positions and can hurt teams with their quality in front of goal!

✗ WEAKNESSES

Even though Rafaelle Souza is one of the world's best defenders, this team's back line isn't the quickest. If they come up against opponents with pace and movement, they could struggle!

VERDICT A great blend of youth and experience in this team, with some key faces in women's football. Marta is considered one of the best of all time!

THE REST OF
┼ GROUP F ┼

Delphine Cascarino

FRANCE

Formation: 4-3-3 Playing style: Solid
Strengths: A excellent back four and lots of pace in attacking areas!
Weaknesses: Some of France's top players are missing out from this year's tournament!
Star player: Delphine Cascarino, Lyon

Khadjia Shaw

JAMAICA

Formation: 4-5-1 Playing style: Give Bunny the ball!
Strengths: Bags of pace, and some promise in midfield from Drew Spence and Trudi Carter!
Weaknesses: A one-woman team, and the defence needs to be much tighter to prevent big defeats!
Star player: Khadija Shaw, Man. City

Marta Cox

PANAMA

Formation: 5-4-1 Playing style: Defensive
Strengths: Panama have been in excellent form against other CONCACAF teams!
Weaknesses: Lacking experience and any real goal threat. Their top scorer has nine goals!
Star player: Marta Cox, Pachuca

SWEDEN

FACT FILE

Nickname: Blagult (The Blue and Yellow)
Manager: Peter Gerhardsson
Captain: Caroline Seger
WWC qualifying: Group A winners
FIFA ranking: 3

WORLD CUP RECORD

BEST RESULT

Runners-up (2003)

IF THEY WERE AN ANIMAL, THEY'D BE...

A REINDEER!

They're used to wintery conditions and work well as a group — but don't mess with them!

SWEDEN FACTS

Greatest ever player: Lotta Schelin
Current league champions: Rosengard
Language: Swedish
Population: 10.4m **Capital:** Stockholm

FORM	★★★★☆
EXPERIENCE	★★★★★
DEFENCE	★★★★☆
ATTACK	★★★★☆
OVERALL	★★★★☆

STAR PLAYER

MAGDALENA ERIKSSON
Club: Chelsea
Position: Defender
Age: 29

STRONGEST LINE-UP!

MUSOVIC

LUNDKVIST BJORN ERIKSSON ANDERSSON

ANGELDAHL ASLLANI ROLFO

KANERYD BLACKSTENIUS JANOGY

FORMATION 4-3-3 PLAYING STYLE DEFENSIVE

✔ STRENGTHS

Sweden have some world-class ballers in their midfield. Barcelona star Fridolina Rolfo and AC Milan captain Kosovare Asllani are their playmakers who'll pull the strings for them!

✘ WEAKNESSES

They've struggled when they've come up against tough attackers, such as England's Alessia Russo. They're well organised, but lacking in creativity and bursts of pace!

VERDICT Sweden have enough talent in their squad for the whole group. They're quick on the ball and technically one of the best on the counter!

THE REST OF + GROUP G +

Estefania Banini

ARGENTINA

Formation: 4-2-3-I **Playing style:** Defensive
Strengths: Some experienced players, like Sole Jaimes, who won the Champions League with Lyon!
Weaknesses: Argentina have struggled getting out of the group stage in recent years!
Star player: Estefania Banini, Atletico Madrid

Cristiana Girelli

ITALY

Formation: 4-3-3 **Playing style:** Possession
Strengths: Packed with talented ballers from Serie A's top clubs, as well as Everton's Aurora Galli!
Weaknesses: Italy simply need to be more clinical in front of goal!
Star player: Cristiana Girelli, Juventus

Thembi Kgatlana

SOUTH AFRICA

Formation: 4-2-3-I **Playing style:** Defensive
Strengths: They won the Women's AFCON last year, so they've had the taste of winning!
Weaknesses: The majority of the team play in in their domestic league, so this will be a huge test!
Star player: Thembi Kgatlana, Racing Louisville

GERMANY

FACT FILE

Nickname: DFB Frauen
Manager: Martina Voss-Tecklenburg
Captain: Alexandra Popp
WWC qualifying: Group H winners
FIFA ranking: 2

WORLD CUP RECORD

BEST RESULT
Champions
(2003, 2007)

IF THEY WERE AN ANIMAL, THEY'D BE...

A DOG!
Powerful, quick and smart — and can be dangerous. Don't expect to outrun them!

GERMANY FACTS
Greatest ever player: Birgit Prinz
Current league champions: Wolfsburg
Language: German
Population: 83.2m **Capital:** Berlin

STAR PLAYER
LEA SCHULLER
Club: Bayern Munich
Position: Forward
Age: 25

FORM	★★★★☆
EXPERIENCE	★★★★★
DEFENCE	★★★★☆
ATTACK	★★★★☆
OVERALL	★★★★☆

STRONGEST LINE-UP!

FROHMS
KLEINHERNE HENDRICH HEGERING RAUCH
MAGULL OBERDORF DABRITZ
HUTH SCHULLER POPP

FORMATION 4-3-3 PLAYING STYLE COUNTER-ATTACKING

✔ STRENGTHS

These players are no strangers to club trophies. The squad is stacked full of quality midfielders from Europe's top clubs who know how to run and control a game at the highest level!

✘ WEAKNESSES

Germany's all-conquering team of the 1990s and early-2000s is now nothing but a distant memory. Have they forgotten how to win on the biggest stage of all?

VERDICT After narrowly losing to England in the final of Euro 2022, this team will be hungrier than ever to go one better and win a third World Cup!

THE REST OF ╋ GROUP H ╋

Catalina Usme

COLOMBIA

Formation: 4-2-3-1 Playing style: Defensive
Strengths: One of South America's strongest teams — they've been in great form in recent matches!
Weaknesses: The defence is easily tested when they come up against stronger opponents!
Star player: Catalina Usme, America De Cali

Rosella Ayane

MOROCCO

Formation: 4-3-3 Playing style: Possession
Strengths: Morocco have been able to dominate up front and use their top scorers wisely in front of goal!
Weaknesses: It's their first World Cup and that lack of experience could cost them dearly!
Star player: Rosella Ayane, Tottenham

Ji So-Yun

SOUTH KOREA

Formation: 3-5-2 Playing style: Defensive
Strengths: Midfielder Ji So-Yun was one of Chelsea's best players — she scored 37 goals in her time there!
Weaknesses: The majority of the squad are lacking in experience outside of the domestic league!
Star player: Ji So-Yun, Suwon

BBC
MATCH
OF THE
DAY
+
MAGAZINE

IWABUCHI

JAPAN

FACT FILE

Full name Mana Iwabuchi
Date of birth 18 March 1993 (age 30)
Place of birth Tokyo, Japan
Position Midfielder **Club** Arsenal

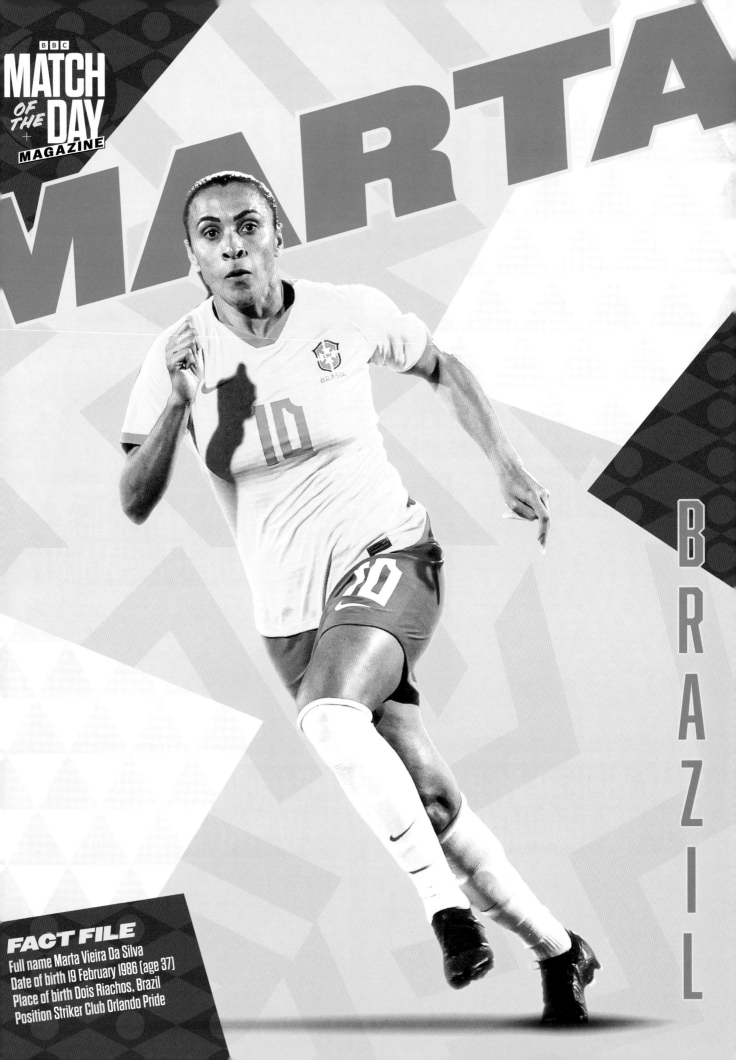

BBC

MATCH OF THE DAY
MAGAZINE

MARTA

BRAZIL

FACT FILE

Full name Marta Vieira Da Silva
Date of birth 19 February 1986 (age 37)
Place of birth Dois Riachos, Brazil
Position Striker Club Orlando Pride

MY 2023 WORLD CUP AWARDS!

Watch the tournament and then make a note of your big winners on this page!

MY PROFILE

NAME

....

....

AGE

....

STICK YOUR PHOTO HERE

MY PLAYER OF THE TOURNAMENT

NAME

....

COUNTRY

....

MY YOUNG PLAYER OF THE TOURNAMENT

NAME

....

COUNTRY

....

MY FAVOURITE NEW PLAYER

NAME

....

COUNTRY

....

MY FAVOURITE GOAL

SCORER

....

COUNTRY

....

OPPOSITION

....

DRAW WHAT HAPPENED BELOW!

MY FAVE WORLD CUP 2023 MOMENT

....
....
....
....
....
....

MY WORLD CUP 2023 TOURNAMENT RATING

0	THE WORST	☐
2	RUBBISH	☐
4	NOT GREAT	☐
6	NOT BAD	☐
8	PRETTY SICK	☐
10	UNBELIEVABLE	☐

BIGGEST SHOCK RESULT

COUNTRY

SCORE
☐

....

V

COUNTRY

SCORE
☐

....

THE WORLD CUP 2023 IN ONE WORD

MY 2023 WORLD CUP DREAM TEAM!

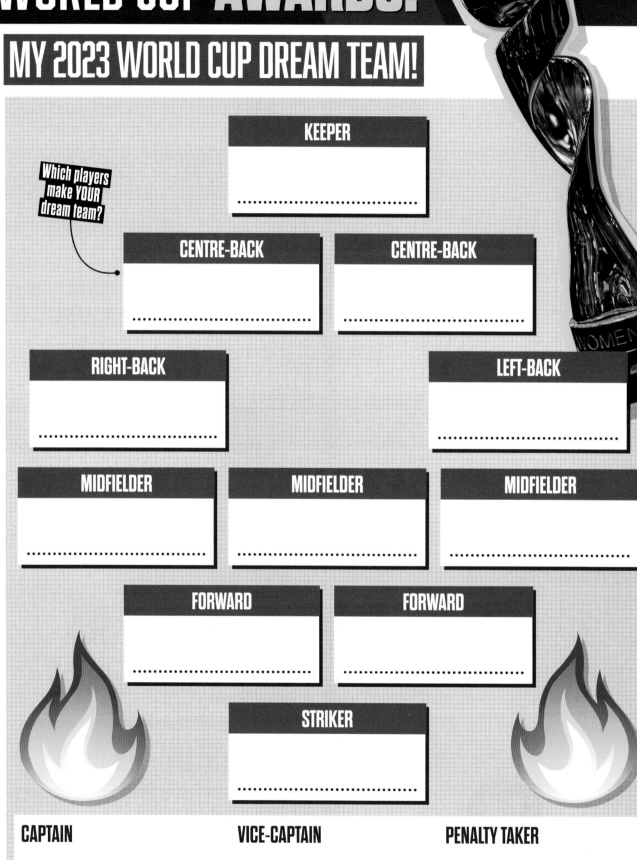

KEEPER

....

Which players make YOUR dream team?

CENTRE-BACK

....

CENTRE-BACK

....

RIGHT-BACK

....

LEFT-BACK

....

MIDFIELDER

....

MIDFIELDER

....

MIDFIELDER

....

FORWARD

....

FORWARD

....

STRIKER

....

CAPTAIN

....

VICE-CAPTAIN

....

PENALTY TAKER

....

FIFA PLAYER OF THE TOURNAMENT

NAME

....

COUNTRY

....

GAMES / GOALS

....

GOLDEN BOOT WINNER

NAME

....

COUNTRY

....

GAMES / GOALS

....

THE BEST MATCH

COUNTRY

SCORE

....

COUNTRY

SCORE

....

THE BEST 2023 WORLD CUP KIT

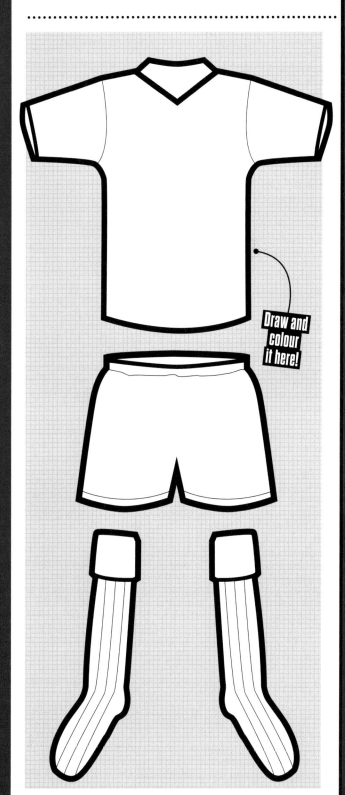

COUNTRY

....

Draw and colour it here!

START SUB SELL!

PICK ONE PLAYER FROM EACH ROW to be in your starting line-up, one to sit on the bench, and one you'd get rid of!

1

Start ☑ Sub ☑ Sell ☑
LAUREN HEMP

Start ☑ Sub ☑ Sell ☑
LAUREN JAMES

Start ☑ Sub ☑ Sell ☑
CHLOE KELLY

2

Start ☑ Sub ☑ Sell ☑
GEORGIA STANWAY

Start ☑ Sub ☑ Sell ☑
JI SO-YUN

Start ☑ Sub ☑ Sell ☑
LENA OBERDORF

3

Start ☑ Sub ☑ Sell ☑
ALESSIA RUSSO

Start ☑ Sub ☑ Sell ☑
SAM KERR

Start ☑ Sub ☑ Sell ☑
KHADIJA SHAW

4

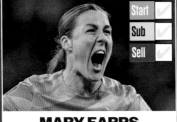
Start ☑ Sub ☑ Sell ☑
MARY EARPS

Start ☑ Sub ☑ Sell ☑
ZECIRA MUSOVIC

Start ☑ Sub ☑ Sell ☑
MERLE FROHMS

5

Start ☑ Sub ☑ Sell ☑
MARTA

Start ☑ Sub ☑ Sell ☑
MEGAN RAPINOE

Start ☑ Sub ☑ Sell ☑
CHRISTINE SINCLAIR

BBC
MATCH
OF
THE
DAY
+
MAGAZINE

RUSSO

ENGLAND

FACT FILE

Full name: Alessia Mia Teresa Russo
Date of birth: 8 February 1999 (age 24)
Place of birth: Maidstone, England
Position: Striker Club: Man. United

WORLD CUP
WHO ARE YA?

Let's see if you can *NAME THESE SIX BALLERS* who'll be balling at the World Cup!

1

A EVE PERISSET
B WENDIE RENARD
C KADIDIATOU DIANI

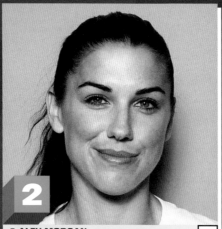

2

A ALEX MORGAN
B ROSE LAVELLE
C CRYSTAL DUNN

3

A LEA SCHULLER
B ALEXANDRA POPP
C ANN-KATRIN BERGER

4

A JILL ROORD
B DANIELLE VAN DE DONK
C LIEKE MARTENS

5

A KATIE McCABE
B AOIFE MANNION
C MEGAN CAMPBELL

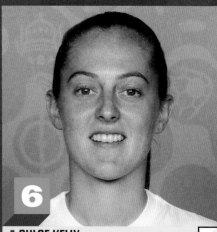

6

A CHLOE KELLY
B RACHEL DALY
C KEIRA WALSH

QUIZ ZONE!

ANSWERS ON p92!

SPOT THE DIFFERENCE!

The USA won the last World Cup in 2019 – but can you find the EIGHT DIFFERENCES between these two photos?

COUNTRY CONUNDRUM!

Can you unscramble the letters below to name the six World Cup 2023 nations?

1 NANA TIGER

....

2 NEWT LIZARDS

....

3 I DETESTS TUNA

....

4 U R A INCREDIBLE FLOP

....

5 BOO CLAIM

....

6 POLAR GUT

....

WORLD CUP QUIZ ZONE!

ANSWERS ON p92!

CROSSWORD!

Use the tricky World Cup clues below to FILL IN THIS GRID!

ACROSS
2 Country captained by Christine Sinclair (6)
7 Australia and Chelsea striker (3, 4)
8 Bayern Munich's Lioness, Georgia _____ (7)
9 Norway captain, _____ Reiten (4)
10 Co-host of the 2023 World Cup (3, 7)

DOWN
1 Club of England stars Lucy Bronze and Keira Walsh (9)
3 Winners of the 2019 World Cup (1,1,1)
4 Sweden striker Stina Blackstenius' club (7)
5 Nickname of Jamaica hotshot Khadija Shaw (5)
6 National team of Debinha and Rafaelle Souza (6)

WHO IS THIS?

Name these two WORLD CUP NATIONS!

MEGASTAR MATCH-UP!

JUST DRAW A LINE from the player to the correct fact!

 1 Marta

 2 Caitlin Foord

 3 Asisat Oshoala

 4 Mary Earps

5 Megan Rapinoe

A She was named in the Euro 2022 Team of the Tournament

B She has won the World Cup and an Olympic gold medal

C She has played for clubs in Australia, USA, Japan and England

D She has been FIFA World Player of the Year six times

E She has won the Golden Boot in Spain and China

WORDSEARCH!

Can you find the five tournament favourites in the grid below?

E	G	S	I	H	T	S
M	E	P	R	Z	H	S
F	R	A	N	C	E	S	S
K	M	I	L	U	T	W
H	A	N	X	S	R	C
E	N	G	L	A	N	D
N	Y	S	X	H	D	Y

FRANCE ✓	USA ✓	SPAIN ✓
GERMANY ✓	ENGLAND ✓	

EMOJI QUIZ!

Can you guess the name of these Lionesses from the EMOJI CLUES BELOW? Just say what you see!

PLAYER 1

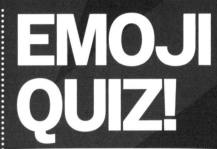

....

PLAYER 2

....

PLAYER 3

....

79

SPOT THE

Uh-oh! The ball has gone missing from the four classic World Cup photo

BALL 1

	A	B	C	D	E	F	G
1							
2							
3							
4							

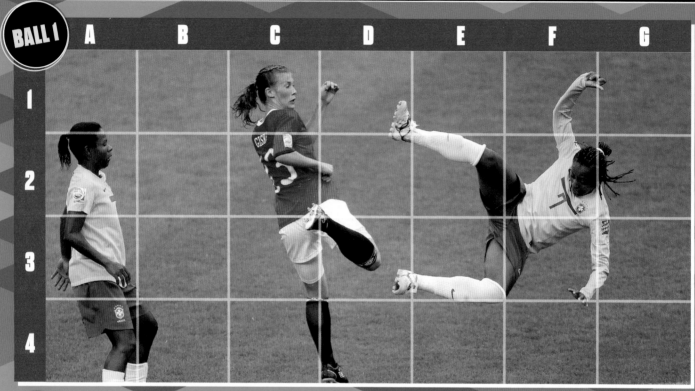

BALL 2

	A	B	C	D	E	F	G
1							
2							
3							
4							

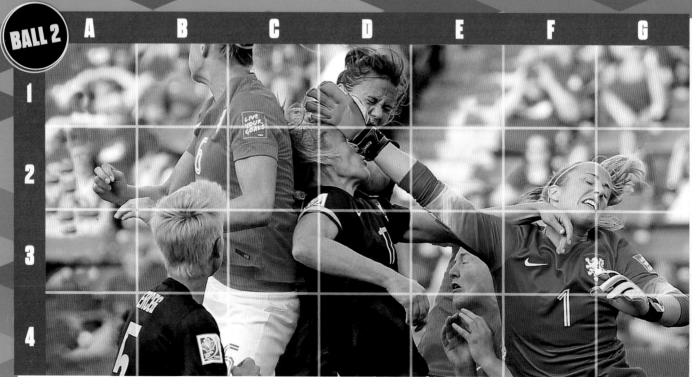

BALL!

ANSWERS ON p92!

...elow – can you guess **WHICH SQUARE IT'S BEEN REMOVED FROM?**

BALL 3

	A	B	C	D	E	F	G
1							
2							
3							
4							

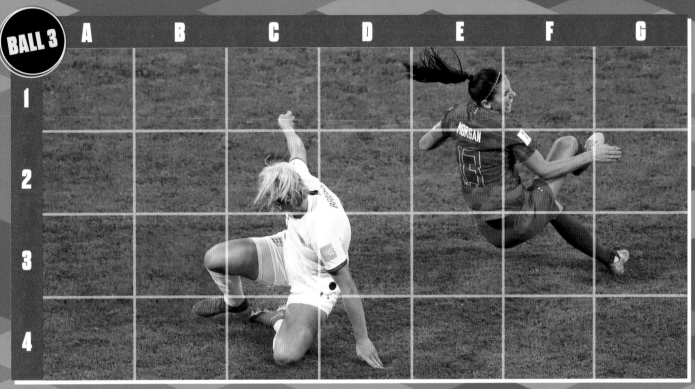

BALL 4

	A	B	C	D	E	F	G
1							
2							
3							
4							

NEVER MISS AN ISSUE OF

BBC

MATCH OF THE DAY MAGAZINE

OFFER DEADLINE DATE 6 JULY 2024

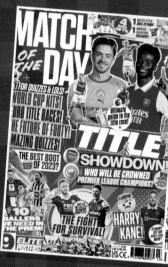   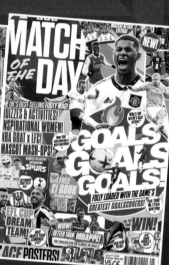

◆ **PAY ONLY £4** *for your first four issues!*

◆ **CONTINUE TO SAVE 10%*** *after your trial!*

◆ **DELIVERY** *direct to your door every issue!*

◆ **NEVER MISS AN ISSUE** *of your favourite footy mag!*

SUBSCRIBE TODAY

VISIT buysubscriptions.com/MDP23L

CALL 03330 162 126† QUOTE MDP23L

BBC
MATCH
OF THE DAY
+ MAGAZINE

KERR

AUSTRALIA

20

FACT FILE

Full name Samantha May Kerr
Date of birth 10 September 1993 (age 29)
Place of birth East Freemantle, Australia
Position Striker Club Chelsea

WOMEN'S FOOTY

USA

NATIONAL WOMEN'S
SOCCER LEAGUE

LEAGUES!

Ultimate guide to the BEST domestic leagues in the world!

ENGLAND
WOMEN'S SUPER LEAGUE

GERMANY
FLYERALARM FRAUEN-BUNDESLIGA

FRAUEN-BUNDESLIGA

FRANCE
D1 FFF ARKEMA

DIVISION I FEMININE

SPAIN
finetwork Liga F

LIGA F

NEWCASTLE

LEEDS

MANCHESTER

LIVERPOOL

BIRMINGHAM

LONDON

ENGLAND

GOVERNING BODY: THE FOOTBALL ASSOCIATION
FOUNDED: 2010
TOP LEAGUE: WOMEN'S SUPER LEAGUE
MAJOR CUP COMPS: FA CUP, LEAGUE CUP

RECORD ATTENDANCE 47,367
Arsenal 4-0 Tottenham, Emirates Stadium, Sep 2022

RECORD GOALSCORER

1 Vivianne Miedema Arsenal **74 GOALS**
2 Bethany England Doncaster Rovers Belles, Chelsea, Liverpool, Tottenham **65 GOALS**
3 Ellen White Arsenal, Notts County, Birmingham City, Man. City **61 GOALS**

CURRENT BEST PLAYER
SAM KERR, CHELSEA

MOST APPEARANCES

1 KERYS HARROP	TOTTENHAM	178 GAMES
2= KATE LONGHURST	WEST HAM	177 GAMES
2= GILLY FLAHERTY	RETIRED	177 GAMES

WSL 2022-23 DREAM TEAM

EARPS MAN. UNITED

BATLLE MAN. UNITED · WILLIAMSON ARSENAL · BRIGHT CHELSEA · LE TISSIER MAN. UNITED

ZELEM MAN. UNITED · MAANUM ARSENAL · McCABE ARSENAL

KERR CHELSEA · DALY ASTON VILLA · SHAW MAN. CITY

MOST TITLES

CHELSEA 5

BIGGEST STADIUM

KING POWER STADIUM LEICESTER, 32,261

TRADITIONAL FOOTBALL STYLE

FAST, PHYSICAL AND DIRECT

TYPICAL HALF-TIME SNACK

MEAT PIE AND BOVRIL

POPULATION 67.75 million
AREA 551,695 km2
CAPITAL Paris CURRENCY Euro
PRESIDENT Emmanuel Macron

PARIS

NANTES

LYON

BORDEAUX

MARSEILLE

NICE

FRANCE

LEAGUE FACTS

RECORD GOALSCORER
Laetitia Tonazzi,
223 goals (2001-18)
MOST APPEARANCES
Gaetane Thiney, 438
games (2000-present)

*CURRENT BEST PLAYER
KADIDIATOU DIANI, PSG*

GOVERNING BODY: FRENCH FOOTBALL FEDERATION
FOUNDED: 1974 TOP LEAGUE: DIVISION 1 FEMININE
MAJOR CUP COMPS: COUPE DE FRANCE,
TROPHEE DES CHAMPIONNES

FRANCE FFF

MOST TITLES	BIGGEST STADIUM	TRADITIONAL FOOTBALL STYLE	TYPICAL HALF-TIME SNACK
OLYMPIQUE LYONNAIS LYON 15	 STADE OCEANE LE HAVRE, 25,000	 *STYLE, STRENGTH AND SKILL*	GALETTE-SAUCISSE A SAUSAGE SANDWICH!

HAMBURG

BERLIN

COLOGNE

FRANKFURT

STUTTGART

MUNICH

GERMANY

GOVERNING BODY: GERMAN FOOTBALL
ASSOCIATION FOUNDED: 1990
TOP LEAGUE: FRAUEN-BUNDESLIGA
MAJOR CUP COMPS: DFB-POKAL

LEAGUE FACTS

RECORD GOALSCORER
Inka Grings, 413 goals
(1995-2014)
MOST APPEARANCES
Kerstin Garefrekes,
365 games (1998-2014)

*CURRENT BEST PLAYER
ALEXANDRA POPP, WOLFSBURG*

MOST TITLES	BIGGEST STADIUM	TRADITIONAL FOOTBALL STYLE	TYPICAL HALF-TIME SNACK

 FRANKFURT 7

 WOLFSBURG 7

DREISAMSTADION
FREIBURG,
24,000

COOL, CALM AND COMPOSED

BRATWURST

BILBAO

BARCELONA

MADRID

VALENCIA

SEVILLE

MALAGA

SPAIN

GOVERNING BODY: ROYAL SPANISH FOOTBALL
FEDERATION FOUNDED: 1988
TOP LEAGUE: LIGA F MAJOR CUP COMPS:
COPA DE LA REINA, SPANISH SUPERCUP

LEAGUE FACTS

RECORD GOALSCORER
Natalia Pablos,
442 goals (2000-13)
MOST APPEARANCES
Priscila Borja Moreno,
419 games (2001-21)

*CURRENT BEST PLAYER
ALEXIA PUTELLAS, BARCELONA*

MOST TITLES	BIGGEST STADIUM	TRADITIONAL FOOTBALL STYLE	TYPICAL HALF-TIME SNACK
 BARCELONA 8	NUEVO COLOMBINO HUELVA, 21,670	*TIKA-TAKA, ONE-TOUCH PASSING*	PIPAS SUNFLOWER SEEDS!

FACT FILE!

POPULATION 331.9 million
AREA 9.834 million km2
CAPITAL Washington, D.C.
CURRENCY U.S. Dollar
PRESIDENT Joe Biden

CHICAGO

NEW YORK

PHILADELPHIA

WASHINGTON

LOS ANGELES

SAN DIEGO

USA

GOVERNING BODY: UNITED STATES SOCCER
FEDERATION FOUNDED: 2012
TOP LEAGUE: NATIONAL WOMEN'S SOCCER LEAGUE
MAJOR CUP COMPS: NWSL CHALLENGE CUP

LEAGUE FACTS

RECORD GOALSCORER
Sam Kerr, 77 goals (2013-19)
MOST APPEARANCES
Lauren Barnes, 189 games (2011-present)

CURRENT BEST PLAYER
ALEX MORGAN, SAN DIEGO WAVE

MOST TITLES	BIGGEST STADIUM	TRADITIONAL FOOTBALL STYLE	TYPICAL HALF-TIME SNACK
PORTLAND THORNS **3**	SNAPDRAGON STADIUM SAN DIEGO WAVE, 32,000	*FAST AND COUNTER-ATTACKING*	 HOT DOG

ANSWERS!

How did you get on with our WORLD CUP QUIZZES?
It's time for you to find out!

FLAG QUIZ

FROM P12

1 B, 2 A, 3 C,
4 C, 5 B, 6 C,
7 A, 8 A, 9 C,
10 A

LIONESS FLASHBACK
FROM P26

1 D, 2 E,
3 G, 4 F,
5 C, 6 B,
7 A

TRUE OR FALSE

FROM P33

1 TRUE,
2 FALSE,
3 FALSE,
4 TRUE,
5 FALSE

LIONESSES QUIZ

FROM P46-47

1 A, 2 C,
3 D, 4 B,
5 D, 6 C,
7 D, 8 A,
9 B, 10 D

WORLD CUP QUIZ ZONE

WHO ARE YA?
1 B, 2 A, 3 B,
4 C, 5 B, 6 C

SPOT THE DIFFERENCE

COUNTRY CONUNDRUM
1 ARGENTINA
2 SWITZERLAND
3 UNITED STATES
4 REPUBLIC OF IRELAND
5 COLOMBIA
6 PORTUGAL

CROSSWORD
FROM P76-79

ACROSS
2 CANADA
7 SAM KERR
8 STANWAY
9 GURO
10 NEW ZEALAND

DOWN
1 BARCELONA
3 USA
4 ARSENAL
5 BUNNY
6 BRAZIL

WHO IS THIS?
NETHERLANDS, GERMANY

MEGASTAR MATCH-UP
1 D, 2 C, 3 E,
4 A, 5 B

WORDSEARCH

E	G	S	I	H	T	S
M	E	P	R	Z	H	S
F	R	A	N	C	E	S
K	M	I	L	U	T	W
H	A	N	X	S	R	C
E	N	G	L	A	N	D
N	Y	S	X	H	D	Y

EMOJI QUIZ
PLAYER 1
LUCY BRONZE,
PLAYER 2 ALEX
GREENWOOD,
PLAYER 3
MILLIE BRIGHT

SPOT THE BALL

FROM P80-81

BALL 1: 1D

BALL 2: 1E

BALL 3: 3B

BALL 4: 1F

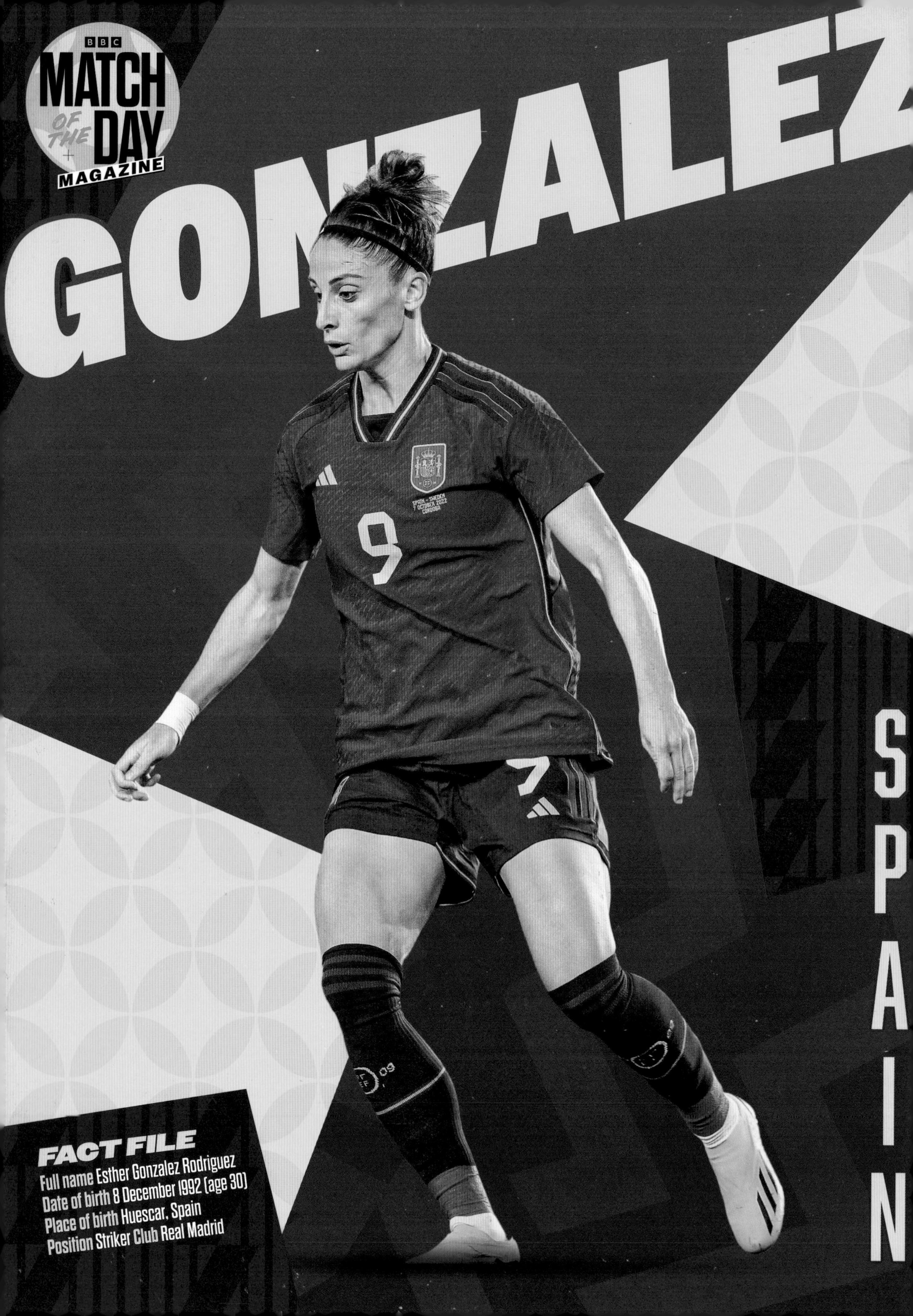

GONZALEZ

SPAIN

FACT FILE

Full name Esther Gonzalez Rodriguez
Date of birth 8 December 1992 (age 30)
Place of birth Huescar, Spain
Position Striker Club Real Madrid